Thomas Kinsella

THE FAMILIAR

Peppercanister 20

Peppercanister

Distributed in Ireland by
The Dedalus Press,
24 The Heath, Cypress Downs, Dublin 6W

in the United Kingdom by
Carcanet Press Limited,
4th Floor, Conavon Court,
12-16 Blackfriars St., Manchester M3 5BQ

in the United States & Canada by
Dufour Editions Inc.,
P.O.Box 7, Chester Springs, Pennsylvania 19425

First published 1999

The Dedalus Press
ISBN 1 901233 36 7 (paper)
ISBN 1 901233 37 5 (bound)

Carcanet Press Ltd
ISBN 1 85754 440 4 (paper)
ISBN 1 85754 439 0 (bound)

Printed in Ireland by Colour Books Ltd.

The Dedalus Press receives financial support from
The Arts Council, An Chomhairle Ealaíon, Dublin.

The Familiar

Love bent the sinewy bow
    against His knee,
saying : *Husband, here is a friend*
    beseeming thee.

Comely Wisdom wearing
    a scarf around Her throat.

CONTENTS

The Familiar

I

I was on my own, fumbling at the neglect
in my attic, up under the roof
over Baggot Street. Remembering
our last furious farewell
— face to face, studying each other
with a hardness like hate.
Mismatched, under the sign of sickness.

My last thoughts alone.
Her knock at the door :
her face bold on the landing.
"I brought you a present."

I lifted in her case.
It was light, but I could tell
she was going to stay.

II

The demons over the door
      that had watched over me
      and my solitary shortcomings

looked down upon us
      going in together
      with our animal thoughts.

III

Muse on my mattress
    with eyes bare
combing her fingers
    down through my hair

Her things on the floor
    a sigh of disorder
box of her body
    in an oxtail odour

Bending above me
    with busy neck
and loose locks
    my mind black

IV

In my night sweat she was everywhere,
feeling : *Come flesh. Come bones.*
And I beat on the body of Love, saying :
Tomorrow. You'll see.

Fire's red flames fading
in a dark room.
Her voice whispering in my ear : *It is all*
right. It is all right.

V

I rose with need in the small hours
and felt my way along the landing
to empty my system beside the sink.

The moon bright
on the three graces above the tank.
The youngest, chosen; stripped and ready.
Her older sister nude behind her,
settling her hair. Their matron mother
to one side, holding the mirror.

I felt my way back afterwards
along the landing, into my place.
Our legs locked in friendship.

VI

I was searching for the lost well-head,
among thick fruits, under leather leaves,
when I beheld a shaft of light

slanting down golden
glistening with seeds,
in a glade humming with pleasure.

On a field *or* :
a decorative flicker.
                    A nymph advancing,

spurning the blades of the grass with little tough feet;
picking the pale-stemmed blossoms in her path;
laying them in the crook of her arm and against her cheek;

her tongue, coral pink, lingering among them;
her hair falling all over them,
tangled with the remains of the morning's floral crown.

Her floral tresses

lifted and swayed,

        whispering : *Come.*

VII

I was downstairs at first light,
looking out through the frost on the window
at the hill opposite and the sheets of frost
scattered down among the rocks.

The cat back in the kitchen.
Folded on herself. Torn and watchful.

*

A chilled grapefruit
— thin-skinned, with that little gloss.
I took a mouthful, looking up along the edge of the wood

at the two crows high in the cold
talking to each other,
flying up toward the tundra, beyond the waterfall.

*

I sliced the tomatoes in thin discs

in damp sequence into their dish;

scalded the kettle; made the tea,

and rang the little brazen bell.

And saved the toast.

                         Arranged the pieces

in slight disorder round the basket,

and fixed our places, one with the fruit

and one with the plate of sharp cheese.

                *

I stood in my dressing gown

with arms extended

over the sweetness of the sacrifice.

Her shade showed in the door. Her voice responded :

"You are very good.

You always made it nice."

St John's

We were outside the high wall,
staying clear of the new entrance.
You were in front, finding the way
along the edge of the Ringwood.

You came to the corner, up to your heart
in the high grass, on the old path
down to the Slaney. We could hear
the new people on the other side.

Ghost hands,
from behind, across your heart.
Your head low
in the confusion of assent.

Wedding Evening

Three women from the North side
were sitting together in the dark
on the Canal wall, by the bridge opposite our house,
at the quiet end of the terrace.

Where she stood this morning
in the front window
in her white veil.
                Sara in certainty.

Iris

On a spear of leaf,
with her wings shivering,

a maiden messenger
whispering detail.

Iris.
    Her frail tail

uplifted, leaving
a virginal drop.

THE FAMILIAR is number 20 in the Peppercanister series by Thomas Kinsella. It is set in 12 point Times New Roman and published in a paperback edition of 1,200 copies and a bound edition of 350 copies.

First published May 1999

The cover design and priest figure are taken from "CELTIC ORNAMENT : Art of the Scribe", by Courtney Davis, (Blandford, UK, 1996.)